CRICKET

Facts, Figures & Fun

*"Any book without a mistake in it has had
too much money spent on it"*

Sir William Collins, publisher

CRICKET

FACTS, FIGURES & FUN

LIAM McCANN

Cricket
Facts, Figures & Fun

Published by
Facts, Figures & Fun, an imprint of
AAPPL Artists' and Photographers' Press Ltd.
Church Farm House, Wisley, Surrey GU23 6QL
info@ffnf.co.uk www.ffnf.co.uk
info@aappl.com www.aappl.com

Sales and Distribution
UK and export: Turnaround Publisher Services Ltd.
orders@turnaround-uk.com
USA and Canada: Sterling Publishing Inc.
sales@sterlingpub.com
Australia & New Zealand: Peribo Pty.
michael.coffey@peribo.com.au
South Africa: Trinity Books. trinity@iafrica.com

A catalogue record for this book is available from the
British Library.

ISBN 13: 9781 904 332 664
ISBN 10: 1 904 332 668

Design (contents and cover): Malcolm Couch
mal.couch@blueyonder.co.uk

Printed in China by Imago Publishing
info@imago.co.uk

CONTENTS

CHAPTER 1
ORIGINS OF THE GAME

THE NAME

It's difficult to trace the origin of the word 'cricket' but it seems that the Anglo-Saxon word for a shepherd's staff in the late Middle Ages was *cricc* or *cryce*. Shepherds would use this staff as a bat while balls made from wood or hide were thrown at the gates of sheep pens, which doubled as primitive wickets (and were sometimes known as wicket-gates). Another possibility is that the bat and ball game *creag* – played by the royal family – evolved into *creag-a-wicket* and thence to cricket. The French word *criquet* (meaning stick or club) appears to predate both croquet and cricket, which may have a common origin.

THE GAME

Whatever the origin of the name, the game itself appears first in southern England, primarily in Sussex, Surrey and Kent. As early as Norman times (*c*1066) a crook was used to deflect a ball (made from sheep's wool) away from a gate or tree stump, though whether the conquering French army brought the game to England or adopted it once they'd arrived remains a mystery. This primitive form of cricket probably developed from the popular pastime of bowls, with a new rule allowing a defender to try and protect the 'jack' by hitting the bowl away.

Bat and ball games can be traced back across Europe into the 9th and 8th centuries. Polo first appeared in India, then migrated to Persia, Constantinople and Europe. Board games such as chess followed a similar route during the same period. It is therefore possible that the first bat and ball games came from the Punjab region in south-east Asia and migrated to Europe in time for the Normans to bring them to England in 1066. The first written evidence of such a game comes from the time of the Plantagenet King Henry II in 1183.

If the game was played between the Norman conquest and the Middle Ages, it was probably only in localised pockets across the south as there are no solid references until 1550. John Derrick of Guildford, Surrey, testified in a dispute over land ownership between the Royal Grammar School in the town centre and a local farmer. Though the inquest was held in 1597, he recalled playing *kreckett* on the land half a century earlier. From then on the game can be traced more accurately, with adults being prosecuted for breaking the Sabbath by playing on a Sunday instead of going to church in 1611. Until then, contemporary accounts held that it was a game played by boys only.

At the end of the English Civil War, and with the death of Charles I in 1649, Oliver Cromwell clamped down on all sports played on the Sabbath. As this was the only time available to the working classes in which to play the game, it moved elsewhere, finding refuge in public schools such as Eton and Winchester. Cromwell visited Ireland in 1656 and, in a statute of the same year issued by the Commissioners of the Lord Protector of England, banned the sport of *krickett*, decreeing that all sticks and balls should be burned henceforth by the local hangman.

Immediately after the restoration of the monarchy cricket began to thrive, and a Gambling Act was passed in 1664 to limit the amount of money that could be wagered on the outcome of matches. Towards the end of the century an eleven-a-side match was played between teams in Sussex with fifty guineas at stake.

The oldest surviving bat dates from 1729, though it resembles a modern ice-hockey stick in size and shape. Bowlers were still obliged to deliver the ball under-arm along the ground in the early 18th century and the broad, flat face of the stick could be used to flick the ball away. Sometime after 1760 bowlers were allowed to lob the ball, allowing it to pitch before the batsman. This gave rise to a new set of tactics, including varying the pace and line of the delivery, as well as applying spin to the ball. Edward Stevens was the first bowler to incorporate these tactics in a match, in 1762, and, as is so often the case during a sport's evolution, the batsmen had to develop new techniques to deal with the threat. John Small adapted his

batting style accordingly, fashioning a straight bat carved from a single piece of wood that enabled him to defend both spinning and faster deliveries.

The first attempt to codify the game was made in 1744. The new laws standardised the pitch dimensions, pop-

W. G. GRACE

Only two men have stood head and shoulders above their contemporaries in the history of cricket. The fabulous Australian batsman Sir Donald Bradman (1908-2001) averaged 99.94 in his Test career – which ran from 1928 to 1948 – nearly double that of all the top players around today. He scored a century every three innings in all first-class matches and remains the first name on any all-time XI team sheet. The second man would be Doctor William Gilbert Grace (1848-1915).

WG, as he was known, popularised the sport for both spectators and participants. In his time he was one of the two most famous Englishmen, the other being Prime Minister William Gladstone. In only his second match, aged just fifteen, he scored 170 and 56 not out, the first remarkable performances in a career that would span nearly half a century. Aged eighteen he proved his all-round ability by scoring 224 not out for an England XI against Surrey in the morning and then winning a quarter-mile sprint at Crystal Palace after lunch. As he grew older his skill and style changed the way cricket was played. He saw the ball early, was a good judge of line and length, had reserves of stamina and

ping crease, wicket size and ball weight (see timeline). From 1756 until MCC (Marylebone Cricket Club) took over in 1787, the Hambledon Club in Hampshire assumed the role of governing body. Their first major rule change concerned limiting the width of the bat to $4\frac{1}{4}$ inches after Thomas White took guard with a bat as wide as the wicket in 1771. These and other laws were

---

concentration, and could play all the shots. This was demonstrated in perhaps his finest innings, 400 not out against 22 fielders.

Pitches were open to the elements until covers were tentatively introduced at Lord's in 1872, and the playing surfaces around the country were notoriously unreliable. As a result centuries were rare. Grace scored 1,000 runs and took 100 wickets in six consecutive seasons (1873-78) and in one week in 1876 hit 344 against Kent, 318 not out against Yorkshire and 177 against Nottinghamshire. In all he scored 54,896 first-class runs (including 126 centuries) and took 2,876 wickets (including 126 catches). In his time he was quite simply incomparable, the first Champion. The Grace Gates at Lord's are named in his honour.

introduced over the next fifteen years until MCC, founded by the Earl of Winchilsea and the Honourable Colonel Charles Lennox, published its definitive list of rules, governing everything from pitch measurements to equipment provided, in 1788.

Indeed by 1790 the traditional method of scoring a game by making notches on a wooden staff had been abandoned for the now familiar score-book. The first man to favour paper and pencil was supposedly Samuel Britcher and he was employed by MCC as a result. Scores up until this point might have simply read: Surrey beat Sussex. The margin of victory (in notches) appeared in results tables around 1730 and each team's overall total came some four years later. Numbers of wickets lost were listed in 1737 and the time of each dismissal appeared shortly afterwards. By 1773 bowlers and fielders were listed by name and position, and the method of dismissal was also recorded.

Cricket was usually seen as a game for the aristocracy, with some wealthy gentlemen hiring commoners to throw gently lobbed balls for them to hit. In London, these games were usually held at White Conduit Fields in Islington. Winchilsea and Lennox were unhappy with the current arrangement over the ground and decided to approach Thomas Lord, a WCCC bowler, who had leased a plot in Dorset Fields. His circle of friends played there without being watched by large sections of the lower classes gathering to place wagers on the outcomes of games. The first match on his turf was played between Middlesex and Essex in 1787. The following year the newly formed MCC played its first game on Lord's ground and defeated White Conduit by 83 runs.

MCC moved from Dorset Fields to Regent's Park in 1811, and in 1814 it moved for the final time to its present home in St John's Wood (after the landlord had increased Lord's rent disproportionately). Thomas Lord died in 1825 and the cricket ground was named in his honour, Lord's being seen as the home of English cricket ever since and one of the finest grounds in the world today. At the time of Lord's death, however, the ground had to be saved by William Ward, with an investment of £5,000.

With the introduction of over-arm bowling came changes in bats and tactics, and ground-staff began to take a more active role, preparing pitches with mowers and rollers so that both sides of the game were able to advance. These innovations allowed for healthy competition (with higher scores and therefore greater crowd interest) and teams representing counties contested an unofficial championship from the mid-1860s.

The first side to tour overseas visited America in 1859, and such was its success that it was soon followed by a tour to Australia (the scheduled tour of America having been cancelled as a result of the Civil War). This gave rise to the Ashes, and international cricket gradually spread across the globe by way of the Commonwealth.

"He only came unstuck against the ball that bowled him"
Simon Metcalf

"England were beaten in the sense that they lost"
Dickie Davis

CRICKET TIMELINE

1300: The Prince of Wales plays a game called *creag* in Newenden, Kent, against his friend Piers Gaveston. Some believe it is a cricket-like sport that evolves into the modern equivalent.

1477: Edward IV bans some outdoor games as they prevent people practicing valuable archery skills.

1523: Stoolball, a likely precursor to rounders, is mentioned in a history of Sussex. *Stool* is the old Sussex word for tree-stump, which may have been used as a wicket.

1550: Cricket (*kreckett*) played in Guildford, Surrey.

1610: Sides from the Weald and the Downs meet for a match at Chevening, Kent.

1676: First instance of the game being played abroad, between ex-pats in Syria.

1709: First county match is played between Kent and Surrey at Dartford Brent.

1710: Cricket played at Cambridge University.

1744: The London Club issues a set of laws. Wickets must measure 22 by 6 inches and the pitch is standardised to 22 yards (a measurement handed down from Saxon times and equal to one tenth of a furrow long [furlong] or the breadth of a strip-acre).

1745: First recorded match between women (Bramley Maids v Hambledon Maids) on Godsen Common, Guildford.

1756: Hambledon Club formed. It remains the home of cricket until MCC and Lord's achieve dominance towards the end of the century.

1760: Bowlers allowed to pitch the ball rather than rolling it along the ground.

1771: The width of the bat set at 4¼ inches. (This has remained unchanged.)

1774: LBW introduced.

1775: 'Lumpy' Stevens's bowling responsible for introduction of third stump.

1787: MCC (Marylebone Cricket Club) formed. Thomas Lord hosts match in Dorset Square, London.

1796: Handicapped games played between wounded servicemen and Greenwich pensioners in Montpelier Gardens, London.

1797: Rules are laid down by the MCC.

1798: Wickets increase in size to 27 by 8 inches.

1800: Christine Willes experiments with over-arm bowling to avoid tangling her arm in her skirt.

1806: First Gentlemen (amateurs) versus Players (professionals) match.

1811: Surrey women play Hampshire women in London.

1814: Lord opens current ground in St John's Wood.

1815: First recorded instance of a side being all out for 0 (Hampton Green).

1827: First Oxbridge match results in a draw.

1830: Runs can still only be scored if the ball is driven in front of the wicket. This practice is exported to North America in 1859 and becomes the foundation for baseball, which survives the First World War whereas cricket does not.

1835: Charles Darwin watches a match between local sides in New Zealand. Pads are introduced.

1836: Bowlers, previously awarded wickets only for clean bowling their victims, are now credited with catches and stumpings.

1837: In the traditional Gentlemen versus Players match, the professionals defend four stumps (36 by 12 inches).

1838: Ball weight set at between five and six ounces, and circumference at nine to nine and a quarter inches.

1844: Canada and the USA contest the first international match (for $1,000) at St George's Club, Hoboken, New Jersey.

1845: The Oval established.

1848: An unnamed bowler takes three wickets with consecutive balls and is presented with a hat with which to collect money from spectators, hence the origin of the word hat-trick.

1850: Gloves issued to the wicketkeeper.

1853: The first willow-bladed, cane-handled bats used.

1857: The first cricket photo taken at the Royal Artillery-Hunsdonbury match.

1864: MCC allows over-arm bowling.

1865: Creases painted rather than dug out.

1877: First Test match between Australia and England in Melbourne is won by the home side.

1880: Australia win the first Test match in England (played at The Oval).

1888: South Africa become third Test playing nation when they take on England at St George's Park, Port Elizabeth.

1889: Option to 'declare' innings closed introduced. South Africa play England in their first Test. Number of balls in an over increased from four to five.

1890: Inaugural county championship.

1896: A two innings, single-wicket match lasts just four balls, a wicket falling with each delivery.

1900: Number of balls in an over upped from five to six. Britain win Olympic gold, the only time cricket has appeared on the program.

1909: Imperial Cricket Conference (ICC) founded by England, Australia and South Africa. This becomes the International Cricket Council.

1910: A 'six' is defined as a hit over the boundary and not out of the ground as it had been previously.

1922: Australia experiments with eight-ball over. New Zealand adopts this in 1924 and South Africa follows suit in 1937.

1928: West Indies acquire Test status. The team consists of islanders from: Anguilla, Antigua and Barbuda, Barbados, Dominica, Grenada, Guyana, Jamaica, Montserrat, St Kitt's & Nevis, St Lucia, St Vincent & the Grenadines and Trinidad & Tobago.

1930: England play their first match against New Zealand.

1931: Stumps increased in height and width by an inch to 28 by nine.

1932: India play England in their first Test. Bodyline tour of Australia sours relations between hosts and England.

1948: Test matches scheduled for five days.

1952: Pakistan play India in their first Test in Delhi.

1963: Inaugural Gillette Cup year. It becomes the first domestic one-day trophy.

1971: Australia beat England by five wickets in the first one-day international in Melbourne.

1975: The first World Cup is held in England.

1977: Australian entrepreneur Kerry Packer signs leading players to World Series Cricket. The split is resolved in 1979.

1979: Australia finally abolishes its eight-ball over in favour of six.

1982: Sri Lanka enters the Test arena.

1992: Zimbabwe granted Test status.

1996: Third umpires given power to assist in run-out and close catch decisions.

2000: Bangladesh play India in their first Test.

2001: Hawk-Eye introduced to explain intricacies of LBW decisions. It is also used as a cricketing training aid.

2003: Twenty20 cricket introduced in England.

2005: England regain the Ashes after sixteen years. Their women's team manage the same feat a few weeks earlier. Brian Lara overtakes Allan Border as the most prolific Test batsman.

2006: South Africa and Australia contest the greatest one-day international in history in Johannesburg. A world record number of runs (872) are scored with the home side clinching victory in the last over. Champion of women's cricket Netta Rheinberg dies. In 2001 the former secretary of the Women's Cricket Association had become the first female to be made an honorary member of the MCC.

RULES OF THE GAME

This is the explanation of the game favoured by some, especially when describing it to an American!

You have two sides, one out in the field and one in. Each man that's in the side that's in goes out, and when he's out he comes in and the next man goes in until he's out. When they are all out, the side that's out comes in and the side that's been in goes out and tries to get those coming in, out. Sometimes you get men still in and not out.

When a man goes out to go in, the men who are out try to get him out, and when he is out he goes in and the next man in goes out and goes in. There are two men called umpires who stay out all the time and they decide when the men who are in are out. When both sides have been in and all the men have been out, and both sides have been out twice after all the men have been in, including those who are not out, that is the end of the game.

Confused? Try these rules instead.

Matches are now contested by two teams of eleven players, with one substitute allowed in case of injury, though he may not bat, bowl or keep wicket. After the toss of a coin, the captain who called correctly will decide whether to bat or field. Now that pitches are covered to protect them from the weather before and during the match, it is common for a side winning the toss to bat, except where the pitch is worn or the weather is overcast. On a worn pitch the ball tends to move around more and can be difficult for the batsmen to read, while overcast or blustery conditions tend to make the ball move more in the air, again causing the batsmen problems.

A team's selection committee will usually try to pick a balanced side. In England, where pitches and weather conditions can be conducive to early seam and swing, as well as spin later on, the line up might comprise five specialist batsmen, an all-rounder (bats and bowls well), a wicketkeeper/batsman, three specialist pace/swing/seam bowlers and a spinner. A similar line up might be picked for tours to Australia, South Africa and the West Indies, but pitches on the sub-continent (India, Pakistan, Sri Lanka and Bangladesh) are usually spinner friendly as the pitches tend to wear easily, which offers more to the slow bowler. In this case a team might prefer to pick more than one spinner at the expense of a specialist fast bowler.

Two umpires will officiate the match from the middle, while a third umpire in the stands is responsible for adjudicating on close run out appeals or contentious catches. A match referee oversees all three. The two middle umpires will inspect the pitch to make sure it is suitable, assess the playing conditions (taking the weather and available light into consideration), count the number of balls in the over, signal runs scored, decide when intervals for lunch or tea are taken and ensure the rules of the game (including inspecting the ball) are adhered to at all times. One umpire stands behind the wicket at the bowler's end so he can a) rule whether the ball bowled was legal, b) make decisions on LBW appeals, close catches and run outs, c) signal to the scorers and d) dismiss batsmen who are out. The second umpire stands at square leg (see pitch below) and will adjudicate on no balls – where height is an issue – and run outs at the striker's end.

THE COMMON UMPIRING SIGNALS

Out: Raised index finger on one hand.

Not out: Call of 'Not out'.

Four runs: Arm waved laterally across the chest.

Six runs: Both arms raised above the head.

Wide ball: Both arms extended horizontally to the side.

Bye: One arm extended above the head.

Leg bye: One arm raised above the head while the other touches the knee.

Ask for the TV replay: Trace a square with both hands.

Introduce power-play: Rotate right arm in a circle.

Cancel the last decision: Touch opposite shoulder with both hands.

THE PITCH

The pitch itself occupies the centre of the ground and is 22 yards (20.12 metres) long by 10 feet (3.05 metres) wide. Two sets of wooden stumps (wickets) mark each end. The pitch is prepared by the ground-staff who try – with rollers and mowers – to ensure that the surface remains flat and true for the duration of the match, and is tended much like a golf green. This is so that neither side gains too great an advantage by bowling last on a deteriorating wicket, though this does sometimes happen.

THE GROUND

A cricket ground consists of the pitch and the outfield. Though they vary in size, the grounds are usually ellipti-

Dimensions of the cricket pitch

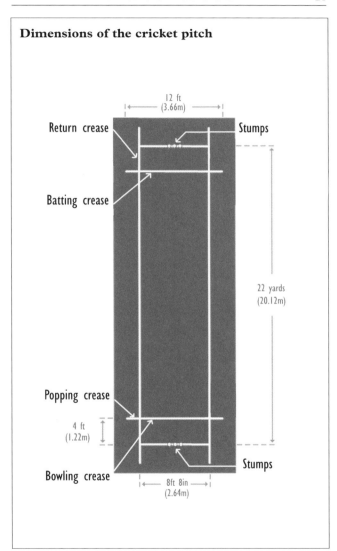

cal (oval), 135-185 metres in length by 110-155 metres in width. If the batsman strikes the ball to the boundary along the ground, he'll be awarded four runs. If he strikes it over the boundary rope without it touching the ground, he'll be awarded six runs. If the ball travels to any other part of the playing surface, the batsmen may choose to run as many as they believe to be safe. The most common shots (and their direction) are shown below:

The fielders may occupy any nine positions on the ground, the two forced upon them being bowler and wicketkeeper. The others are shown opposite.

THE BALL

In men's cricket the ball must weigh between 5½ and 5¾ ounces (156-163g) and must measure between 8 $^{13}/_{16}$ and 9 inches (224-229mm) in circumference. (In women's cricket the ball is some half an ounce lighter and half an inch less in circumference, while in junior cricket it is a further quarter of an ounce and quarter of an inch smaller.) It comprises a cork centre and rubber surround, which are both wrapped in twine and then sealed within four leather quarter-pieces (usually dyed red for Test

Main fielding positions on the cricket pitch
(for a right-handed batsman)

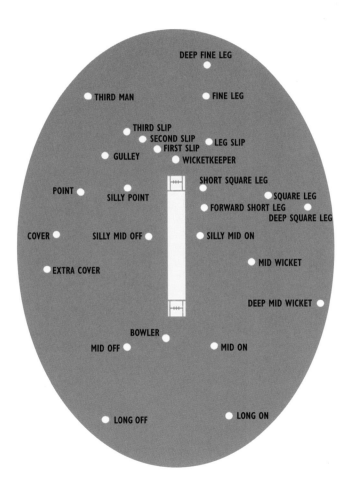

matches and white for one-day matches). It has a
stitched, raised seam about its 'equator', which can help
one side to remain smooth while the other is scuffed
by the bat. This wear and tear on the hemispheres can
make the ball swing in flight (by virtue of differences in
air pressure creating lateral 'lift').

In a Test match the ball is replaced with a new one at the
beginning of each innings and after a certain number of
overs – which varies around the world but is never less
than 75 – at the request of the fielding captain. If the ball
is lost or becomes damaged during play the umpires will
replace it with one in a similar condition.

THE BAT

The overall length of the bat should not exceed 38
inches (965mm), while the blade should have a maximum width of 4¼ inches (108mm). The blade must be
made of wood (usually from the Cricket-bat Willow) but
may be covered with non-abrasive material for its
protection (usually linseed oil). A sprung – but solid –
v-shaped wooden splice connects the handle to the blade.
A bat typically weighs (depending on player preference)
2 lb 8 oz to 3 lb (1.1-1.4 kg), though there are no rules
governing this.

THE STUMPS

There are three stumps at each end of the wicket. They
are 28 inches (711mm) tall and occupy a space 9 inches
(229mm) wide. Balanced (not attached) on top are two
bails, one of which must be dislodged if a batsman is to
be given out bowled, stumped, hit wicket or run out.

OTHER EQUIPMENT

With modern fast bowlers hurling the ball down the pitch at up to 100 mph, it is no surprise to find the batsman being offered some protection. Aside from the bat, he is equipped with pads for the lower legs, thigh pads for the upper legs, arm guards, gloves, a chest protector, helmet, and a reinforced plastic box for the groin. Close in fielders, such as those at short leg, may be issued with similar protection, while the wicketkeeper has padded gloves.

METHODS OF DISMISSAL

There are ten ways of getting out in cricket, the first five of which are, in order of the most to least common: Caught, LBW, bowled, run out and stumped. The five rarer dismissals are, in no particular order: Hit wicket, handled the ball, hitting the ball twice, obstructing the field and timed out (taking more than three minutes to reach the middle). England captain Graham Gooch was famously given out for handling the ball against the Australians in 1993 at Old Trafford, but the first to be timed out was Hemulal Yadav for Indian regional side Tripura in 1997. Sir Len Hutton is the only man to have been given out for obstructing the field in a Test match (against South Africa in 1951), though Pakistan's Ramiz Raja (versus England, 1987), India's Mohinder Amarnath (against Sri Lanka, 1989) and Pakistan's Inzamam-ul-Haq (against India, 2006) all managed it in one-day games. (Shane Warne, Dominic Cork and Graham Thorpe have been given out hit wicket.) In most cases, the fielding side must appeal by shouting *"How's that!"* for the umpire to consider giving the batsman out.

BOWLED

Professional cricketers (top order batsmen in particular) tend not to get bowled very often. Judging the line and length of a delivery, as well as having an innate knowledge of exactly where the stumps are, mean that the best batsmen are able to protect them. But if a ball does sneak through and dislodges the bails, the innings is over. It is very rare, happening once during the 2005 Ashes series, that the ball will strike the stumps but not dislodge the bails and the batsman survives.

CAUGHT

Being caught is the most common way to get out and this type of dismissal accounts for approximately 50-60% of Test match wickets. The catch doesn't have to be taken directly from the bat – a glove will do – but the ball must not touch the ground before being taken.

LBW

Of the methods of dismissal, perhaps the most complex is LBW (leg before wicket). If there is an appeal for LBW, the umpire must consider whether the ball would have gone on to hit the stumps if it hadn't connected with a part of the batsman's body, usually the legs. The umpire should give the batsman 'out' if a) the ball strikes the pad in line with the stumps, provided it did not pitch outside the line of leg stump or b) if the batsman is struck on the pad outside the line of off stump and is not making any attempt to play a shot.

The umpire should give the batsman 'not out' if a) the batsman hits the ball with the bat before it hits the pad or b) if the ball pitches outside leg stump regardless of where it would have gone afterwards or c) the batsman makes a genuine attempt to hit the ball even though it hits him outside the line of off stump or d) if a no-ball has been bowled. The umpire must also consider what height the ball would have bounced, as it will often clear the stumps, and how far down the pitch the batsman was, as this makes it more difficult to judge where the ball would have gone.

RUN OUT

Run outs are more common in limited overs matches. If, while the batsmen are attempting to score a run, the fielding side disturb the bails with the ball while one of the batsmen is out of the crease (i.e. no part of bat or body is grounded behind the line), the umpire should give the player 'out' (unless they are avoiding a dangerous throw, which might have injured them). As the action can be fast and furious the umpires now have the option to refer a close decision to a third umpire who has the benefit of the television replays.

STUMPED

Being stumped is a similar dismissal to being run out, the difference being that the batsmen are not attempting to run. Instead, the player facing the ball has strayed too far down the wicket and is out of his crease. If the wicket-keeper catches the ball and then removes the bails before the batsman has returned to the crease, he will be given out.

HIT WICKET

This kind of dismissal usually occurs when a batsman steps back onto his stumps when trying to avoid a bouncer or yorker (short or full delivery).

DOUBLE HIT

If a batsman deliberately hits the ball twice he can be given out. The exceptions occur when he prevents a ball rolling back onto the stumps after playing it into the ground, or if he is simply returning it to the fielding side.

OBSTRUCTING THE FIELD

If a batsman defends his stumps from a possible run out or deliberately obstructs a fielder attempting to make a catch he can be given out.

HANDLED THE BALL

If the batsman feels the ball might roll or fall onto his stumps he may defend them with his bat or feet, but not his hands. If the player knocks the ball away with the gloves the fielding side will appeal for the dismissal to be given, as two England captains have discovered.

TIMED OUT

A new batsman has three minutes to make it to the crease after a dismissal or the fielders can appeal for the player to be given timed out, but this is extremely rare. England's David Steele got lost on his way to the middle during the 1975 Ashes Test at Lord's but managed to find his way out of the basement toilets just in time!

RETIRED HURT AND RETIRED 'OUT'

If a batsman is injured he may retire hurt, but he's not technically 'out' as he may return to the field if the injury is not deemed too serious. However, a batsman who refuses to bat on (for whatever reason), or is refused permission to bat by the opposing captain (if he has a good enough reason), may be given 'retired out'. It is not listed as an eleventh way of being out because the law is so ambiguous.

"The Port Elizabeth ground is more of a circle than an oval – it's long and square"
Trevor Bailey

"It's his second finger, technically his third"
Christopher Martin-Jenkins

"I don't think I've ever seen anything quite like that before, and it's the second time it's happened today"
Brian Johnston

"He's got his hands up in the middle of his arms"
Nasser Hussain

"Vengsarkar taking a simple catch at square leg, the ball literally dropping down his throat"
Bob Willis

CHAPTER 2
TEST CRICKET

In the 1830s William Clarke, one of Nottinghamshire's first professional cricketers, realised the value in organising a touring 'England' side that would take on both club and county sides nationwide. He made his debut aged just seventeen in 1816 and only retired some forty years later. He became licensee of the Trent Bridge Arms in the early 1830s and opened the ground of the same name in 1837. By 1846 he had formed his All England XI touring side (composed of the best county players) and they played their first match against twenty men of Sheffield later that summer. Although they lost, the idea of local club sides taking on a star-studded outfit was appealing to the masses. So popular were the games that Clarke could afford to pay his players £4 per match. He'd proved to the powers that controlled the game that, if managed properly, touring could turn a tidy profit.

In 1850 MCC became increasingly concerned that the All England team would rival their dominance of the game and its rules at home. A fixture clash in 1854 highlighted the problem. The All England XI were due to play Maidstone on the same day as the annual Gentlemen versus Players match and Clarke refused to release some of his team. By 1852 other stars had launched their own rival England XIs but the novelty of playing county minnows soon wore off, especially as the teams were no longer exclusively made up of celebrities.

Despite the fact that the All England experiment failed, the stars brought their batting, bowling and fielding skills to the village greens and the correct techniques were passed on to generations of younger players. In 1859 a representative England side toured North America – with one match attracting a crowd of 25,000 – and the players returned to England considerably better off, the average take-home earnings being about £90. The tour was a success on the field too, with William Caffyn's sixteen for 25 against New Jersey a high point in a winning cause. Their second match was against Philadelphia – a team that would go on to tour England twice in the 1880s – which they also won. The game in America was destined to fail, however. The Civil War prevented ground-staff tending the pitches and a shortage of materials halted the manufacture of the correct equipment and clothing. Baseball was less reliant on a good pitch or state-of-the-art gear and it flourished as a semi-professional activity amongst the troops. England teams would have to look elsewhere for competition in the future.

County cricket had become increasingly popular throughout the early and mid-nineteenth century. But for cricket to become the global sport idealised by the MCC, the next step was to export the game to the colonies. H. Stephenson captained the first side to tour Australia in 1861-62, taking with him the style of batting learned from the ex-England players still at Surrey. A crowd of 15,000 watched the first match at the MCG and within fifteen years the colonials were capable of beating the mother country at its own game. Test cricket had arrived. The word itself seems to derive from the thought that the game would be a 'test of strength' for the sides, and was first coined relating to the English team that toured Australia in the 1860s. In 1877 James Lillywhite was charged with assembling an All England Test XI to take on Australia in a series in their own country.

England toured South Africa for the first time in 1888-89, playing the first Test in Port Elizabeth, which England won comfortably. South Africa's introduction to the Test arena was more a baptism of fire (that lasted for nearly twenty years), but they finally beat England in a match in 1906 and went on to take that series 4-1. The victorious team then toured England the following year.

Cricket appeared on the list of events for the 1896 Olympic Games in Athens but there weren't enough teams to warrant a competition. The sport made it onto the itinerary for Paris 1900 but still only two teams could be persuaded to take part. Great Britain beat hosts France in the match and were awarded the gold medal. The team still holds the title of Olympic Champions as the sport has not been contested at the Games since.

Until recently cricket satisfied all but one of the criterion for entry into the Games and, contrary to popular opinion, had plenty of countries willing to contest the medals. The reason it had not been included on the program for a century was because both the men's and women's versions of the sport weren't administered by a single governing body, which, in the men's case was the ICC. However, after Australia had won the eighth women's World Cup in South Africa in April 2005, the ICC and IWCC decided to merge to promote the development of the sport among both sexes. The International Olympic Committee (IOC) may now consider including cricket in future Games, particularly the London 2012 event.

The West Indies became the fourth team to be established globally when they took on England at Lord's in 1928. But it would take another two years before the islanders registered their first Test win, the third Test of the home series at Georgetown. A tour of Australia the following

year cemented their place among the elite, though they
wouldn't face South Africa until after apartheid in 1992.
Sides from New Zealand and India emerged in the 1930s
though they took some time to record wins over the established nations, India taking some twenty years to beat
England. Pakistan scored a win in just their second
match, however, that against India in 1952.

As the game grew the Imperial Cricket Conference –
which became the International Cricket Conference
(ICC) in 1965 – realised it would need to broaden its
appeal to emerging cricket nations such as the USA,
Malaysia and Argentina, and it organised all-star tours
there with players like Garry Sobers to attract the crowds.
Unfortunately, the South Africans were heading in the
opposite direction. In 1970 the ICC voted to suspend the
country as a result of its Republican government's
apartheid policy and all tours were cancelled. Sadly this
meant that Test cricket was denied South Africa's prodi-
giously talented players Graeme Pollock and Barry
Richards at the peak of their powers. Several 'rebel' tours
did visit in the 1970s but they were largely composed of
players who were near retirement and wouldn't be affected by sanctions imposed when they returned. Graham
Gooch bucked the trend and led a side there in 1981, but
he was subsequently banned from playing for England for
three years. Generous financial incentives offered by the
South Africans softened the blow.

   With the collapse of the oppressive regime in 1991,
South Africa was immediately reinstated as a Test-playing
nation. Though they narrowly lost their one-day international and Test match returns, players like Allan Donald
and Hansie Cronje proved that their domestic game was
still strong.

WORLD SERIES CRICKET

England captain Tony Greig and Australian media tycoon
Kerry Packer hatched a plan to pay cricketers a percent-
age of gate receipts and broadcasting rights to play in
their own international cricket competition. Players were
poorly paid at the time and most held down jobs that prevented them from training and getting the best out of
themselves, so most players approached by Greig agreed
to join the World Series revolution. The West Indians in
particular jumped at the chance to play professional
cricket as their salaries were so low. Clive Lloyd, Viv
Richards and Andy Roberts accepted three year contracts
worth A$90,000, all believing that further negotiations
would allow them to retire comfortably when the time
came.

The first few matches were poorly attended but mass
media exposure gradually paid off and crowds increased
dramatically. In fact the Packer circus revitalised the sport
(see one-day innovations) and led to Test cricket entering
the modern, professional era with central contracts and
player protection. The experiment didn't last, however.
His point made, and the game changed – most would
agree for the better – Packer dissolved the series in 1979.
The ICC has since ruled that statistics and records from
the series are not to be included in a player's career
figures.

Test cricket remains a popular spectator and television
audience attraction. Despite Australia's dominance for
the last decade there is hope that even the minnows of
Bangladesh and Zimbabwe can now provide a stern test
for the top teams. England's triumph in the 2005 Ashes
precipitated a mass gravitation to the sport, particularly
amongst young people and women. And recent Test series
between India and the West Indies, and England and Sri

HIGHEST INDIVIDUAL TEST SCORES

Name	Score	Venue/Date
Brian Lara (WI)	400*	St John's,Antigua, 2004
Matthew Hayden (Aus)	380	WACA,Perth, 2003
Brian Lara (WI)	375	St John's,Antigua, 1994
Garry Sobers (WI)	365*	Kingston,Jamaica, 1958
Len Hutton (Eng)	364	The Oval,London, 1938
Sanath Jayasuriya (SL)	340	Colombo,Sri Lanka, 1997
Hanif Mohammad (Pak)	337	Bridgetown,Barbados, 1958
Wally Hammond (Eng)	336	Eden Park,Auckland, 1933
Mark Taylor (Aus)	334*	Arbab Niaz,Peshawar, 1998
Don Bradman (Aus)	334	Headingley,Leeds, 1930

* Not Out

Lanka prove that the game has strength in depth and will continue to attract new fans.

"All the ones here. England are 111 for 5"
Nasser Hussain

"I hope no one's house is burning down. It's much too nice a day to be left without a house"
Henry Blofeld

Five players have scored more than 10,000 Test runs: Brian Lara leads the way with 11,505; Allan Border has 11,174; Steve Waugh has 10,927; Sachin Tendulkar has 10,469 and Sunil Gavaskar has 10,122. Lara and Tendulkar are still playing.

Opponents	Duration	Boundaries 6s/4s	Career Test Runs	Career Average
England	12hrs 58mins	4/43	11,505	52.05
Zimbabwe	10hrs 22mins	11/38	7,326	53.08
England	12hrs 46mins	0/45	11,505	52.05
Pakistan	10hrs 14mins	0/38	8,032	57.78
Australia	13hrs17mins	0/35	6,971	56.67
India	13hrs 19mins	2/36	6,745	41.12
West Indies	16hrs 10mins	0/24	3915	43.98
New Zealand	5hrs 18mins	10/34	7,249	58.45
Pakistan	12hrs	1/32	7,525	43.49
England	6hrs 23mins	0/46	6,996	99.94

It's a Funny Old Game: I

South Africa's 1931-32 tour of Australia was dominated by the home side's remarkable batsman Don Bradman. In the first four Tests he scored two double hundreds – including a magnificent 299 not out – and two hundreds. He'd also scored heavily for New South Wales against the tourists (135 and 219) in matches before the fifth and final Test at Melbourne. There the visitors must have been delighted to hear the news that Bradman had tripped on a mat in the dressing room and sprained his ankle and was unable to play. But you'd have thought they would have preferred to score more than 36 in their first innings and 45 in their second. Australia's first innings 153 was enough to give them the match in a Test that lasted less than a single day!

In 1939 South Africa hosted England in a timeless test in Durban. Such was the quality of the wicket that the home side scored 530 to England's 316 in the first innings. Then they rattled up 481 in their second to give the visitors a target of 696 for victory, the game having already lasted for six days. By the end of the week England had reached 253 for one but the next day it rained. Bill Edrich's ninth day 219 seemed likely to set England up for victory and Wally Hammond's 140 took them to 654 for five. Then the rain came and the match was abandoned, the England team having to rush to Cape Town to catch their boat home.

Two Test matches have resulted in ties: West Indies versus Australia in 1961 and Australia against India in 1987.

In 1964 a Commonwealth touring side played a Malaysian XI in Kuala Lumpur. The Commonwealth's star player was undoubtedly Garry Sobers who came to the crease with the score at 68 for one. A huge crowd had gathered expecting to see the great man flay the bowling to all corners but he was undone first ball by beautiful leg-break from Alex Delilkan. Sobers felt he owed the crowd something and delivered in spades with the ball in hand, taking five wickets in five balls!

Still smarting from defeat against India, particularly their spinners, in the third Test in 1976, West Indian captain Clive Lloyd changed tactics and went for all-out attack in the fourth Test by picking a pace quartet of Holding, Daniel, Holder and Julien. India were forced to declare their first innings at six down because captain Bishen Bedi felt that the uneven bounce could result in injuries to his bowlers. West Indies managed close to 400 and then reduced India to 97 for five in their second innings.

THE UMPIRES

Number of Tests – Debut match
One-day Intenationals – Debut match

Steve Bucknor (Jamaica)
113 Kingston (1989) West Indies v India
148 St John's Antigua (1989) West Indies v India

Darrell Hair (Australia)
76 Adelaide (1992) Australia v India
124 Adelaide (1991) India v West Indies

Brent 'Billy' Bowden (NZ)
37 Auckland (2000) New Zealand v Australia
96 Hamilton (1995) New Zealand v Sri Lanka

Aleem Dar (Pak)
34 Dhaka (2003) Bangladesh v England
70 Gujranwala (2000) Pakistan v Sri Lanka

Rudi Koertzen (SA)
77 Port Elizabeth (1992) South Africa v India
154 Port Elizabeth (1992) South Africa v India

Harold 'Dickie' Bird (Eng)
66 Headingley (1973) England v New Zealand
92 Old Trafford (1973) England v New Zealand

Simon Taufel (Australia)
38 MCG (2000) Australia v West Indies
96 SCG (1999) Australia v Sri Lanka

David Shepherd (Eng)
92 Old Trafford (1985) England v Australia
172 Swansea (1983) Pakistan v Sri Lanka

Srinivasaraghavan Venkataraghavan (India)
73 Kolkata (1993) India v England
52 Jaipur (1993) India v England

When no one else appeared at the crease, it soon became apparent that none of the Indian tail were fit to bat, six of their squad suffering broken bones and various other injuries, three of these – to Gaekwad, Patel and Amarnath – so serious that they required hospital treatment.

With India needing 24 runs to avoid the follow-on against England at Lord's in 1990, Kapil Dev smashed Eddie Hemmings for four consecutive sixes.

Day two of the 2000 Lord's Test between the West Indies and England served up a world first. Courtney Walsh was dismissed first ball and the 'Windies' were all out for 267. Then England were skittled for 134 in reply. Then came two of the most remarkable hours of Test cricket. Andrew Caddick charged in and took five for 16 and, backed up by Darren Gough and Dominic Cork, sent the West Indies back to the pavilion with just 54 on the board. England then began their run chase for victory before the close of play, the first time in Test cricket history that part of all four match innings had been played on the same day.

Australian Wayne Phillips and England's Andrew Strauss and Paul Collingwood have all been given out in a Test match having played the ball down on to a boot and then having it leap into the air for a catch to be taken. Phillips hit Allan Lamb on the foot before David Gower pouched the ball, while the latter two played the ball off their own feet and were caught at short leg.

TALKING BALLS I

"The Queen's Park Oval, exactly as its name suggests, is absolutely round"
Tony Cozier

"The only possible result is a draw. The alternative is a win for England"
Richie Benaud

"With his lovely soft hands he just tossed it off"
Bobby Simpson

"Harmison likes to play every shot in the book, sometimes to the same ball"
Charles Colville

"That's what cricket is all about: two batsmen pitting their wits against one another"
Fred Trueman

"His throw went absolutely nowhere near where it was going"
Richie Benaud

"In Hampshire's innings, the Smith brothers scored 13 and 52 respectively"
Henry Blofeld

"That slow-motion replay doesn't show how fast the ball was travelling"
Richie Benaud

LEADING TEST WICKET TAKERS

Name	Matches	Wickets
Shane Warne (Aus)	140	685
Muttiah Muralitharan (SL)	108	657
Glenn McGrath (Aus)	119	542
Courtney Walsh (WI)	132	519
Anil Kumble (India)	110	533
Kapil Dev (India)	131	434
Richard Hadlee (NZ)	86	431
Wasim Akram (Pak)	104	414
Curtly Ambrose (WI)	98	405
Shaun Pollock (SA)	102	395
Ian Botham (Eng)	102	383

SLEDGING

Sledging is the art of verbally intimidating a batsman so that he loses his concentration and gets himself out. It is also known as the art of initiating mental disintegration. The fielders will use a variety of tactics to do this, including: the witty welcome to the crease, the loud chirp from the wicketkeeper, the behind-the-back shout, the unexpected question or observation (which may be aggressive or shocking and have nothing to do with cricket), the sarcastic taunt, and the send off, the latter seeing the departing batsman ushered from the pitch, a volley of abuse ringing in his ears. The word itself appears to derive from the observation that New South Wales cricketer Grahame Corling was as subtle as a sledgehammer having offended his host at a party.

Best Innings Bowling	Opponents	Venue / Date
8-71	England	Brisbane / 1994
9-51	Zimbabwe	Kandy / 2001-02
8-24	Pakistan	Perth / 2004
7-37	New Zealand	Wellington / 1995
10-74	Pakistan	Delhi / 1998-99
9-83	West Indies	Ahmedabad / 1983
9-52	Australia	Brisbane / 1985
7-119	New Zealand	Wellington / 1994
8-45	England	Barbados / 1990
7-87	Australia	Adelaide / 1998
8-34	Pakistan	Lord's / 1978

It is commonly believed that the Australian sides of the 1970s and '80s started this underhand tactic, but the father of rule bending was, in fact, the Champion of English cricket at the end of the 19th century, Doctor W.G. Grace. There are numerous stories about  the great man using every possible tactic, legal and otherwise, to win. In one match he pointed at a flock of birds just as they flew across in front of the sun. Sensing that the batsman had been dazzled by the sunshine, Grace sent down one of his quicker balls and clean bowled him.

In another instance he was bowled himself first ball. The mood of the crowd changed for the worse because they'd been forced to pay a sixpence entry fee instead of the usual three just because Grace was playing. The doctor didn't disappoint, however. He simply replaced the bails and chastised the bowler with:

"They've come to see me bat, young man, not to watch you bowl."

Here are a select few of the printable sledges and replies that have graced the Test match arena:

Disgraced South African captain Hansie Cronje was involved in one of the game's great moments. He'd been demolishing Mervyn Hughes's bowling while the Australians were on tour in the early '90s and big Merv was getting pretty fed up. Having watched the ball sail over the boundary rope yet again, he headed down to Cronje, let out a rumbling fart, and said:

"Try hitting that for six."

This next quote is pure Viv Richards, though it has been attributed to any number of batsmen since, such is its universal appeal. Glamorgan's Greg Thomas hurled down a wicked out-swinger that beat the Somerset legend all ends up. The pace-man quipped:

"It's red and round and weighs about five ounces. Can't you see it?"

There's nothing like teeing yourself up for a fall. Richards got hold of the next ball, smashing it into the river outside the ground. Seeing the stunned look on Thomas's face, he replied:

"You know what it looks like. Go get it!"

There was a degree of hostility between Australian wicket-keeper Ian Healey and portly Sri Lankan batsman Arjuna Ranatunga that continued throughout their careers. Shane Warne was becoming frustrated with the Sri Lankan because he couldn't get him out, so he asked Healey for his suggestions on how to draw Ranatunga out of his crease. Healey replied:

"Put a Mars Bar on a good length. That should do it."

Ranatunga is said to have pointed at David Boon at short leg and replied:

"Don't bother, Boonie will be onto it well before I can move."

In 2002 South African captain Graeme Smith revealed that he'd been verbally abused by the touring Australians and this prompted outbursts from the rest of his team, who recounted their own stories of bullying from the middle. The media went into overdrive, with the South African press giving the Australian team a roasting and the Australian camp spinning their lines to minimise the damage. The Aussies were eventually forced to contribute to the 2003 document entitled *The Spirit of Cricket*, an excerpt of which is printed below:

"We do not condone or engage in sledging or any other conduct that constitutes personal abuse. We view positive play, pressure, body language and banter between opponents and ourselves as legitimate tactics and integral parts of the competitive nature of cricket."

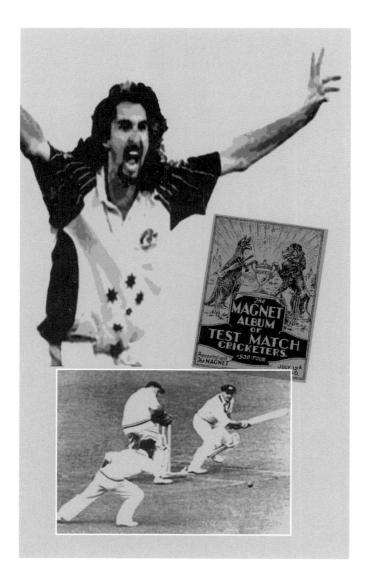

CHAPTER 3
THE ASHES

With the MCC looking to promote the game abroad, James Lillywhite was charged with taking cricket to the colonies on the 1877 tour of Australia. After a long journey by sea, the two sides lined up at the Melbourne Cricket Ground (MCG) on 15th March. Home batsman Charles Bannerman became the first Test match centurion when he scored a first innings 165. Australia went on to win by 45 runs, a result that stunned the tourists as they had been expected to win comfortably. England won the return match a couple of weeks later and the series was tied at 1-1.

The home side won the only Test match – played at the MCG – on England's 1878-79 Lord Harris led tour, thanks largely to the bowling of Fred Spofforth who took 13-110 in the match (which included the first international hat-trick). The tourists' captain was so disappointed in his own performance that he hurled his bat across the pavilion. The bad feelings rolled over to an unofficial re-match in Sydney, and when Australian umpire George Coulthard adjudged local hero Billy Murdoch run out, two thousand spectators invaded the pitch and began attacking the English players. Lord Harris was beaten with a whip, Albert Hornby had his shirt ripped and the other English players were forced to defend themselves with stumps. In retaliation, many English clubs refused to play the touring Australians when they visited the following year.

Both sides won a series before the Australians toured England in 1882. By then the two teams had contested nine Test matches, with Australia winning five and England two, there being two draws. The single Test match at The Oval in August turned into tense affair of few runs. England needed just 85 in their second innings to win and had cruised to 51 for two, but then the pressure began to tell. They lost a couple of wickets and then the last five fell for just seven runs, leaving England all out on 77, eight short of their target.

Then the Ashes legend was born, the contest finding its name in the words of a mock obituary penned by Reginald Brooks in the *Sporting Times*. The young reporter had just witnessed England lose the Test match in a nail-biting finish, their first defeat by the tourists on home soil:

> *In affectionate remembrance of English cricket*
> *which died at The Oval on 29 August, 1882.*
> *Deeply lamented by a large circle of sorrowing friends and*
> *acquaintances, R.I.P.*
> *N.B. The body will be cremated and the ashes taken to*
> *Australia.*

This prompted the press to hype up England's 1882-83
tour to Australia, forcefully making the point that the
Honourable Ivo Bligh's team should return home with
the Ashes. (When Bligh mentioned this in a speech in
Adelaide after the tourists' warm-up game, the locals had
no idea what he was talking about. The obituary had not
been printed in Australia.)

There are two conflicting stories of how the famous urn
came to hold and symbolise the Ashes. The first has it that
the urn held the remains of a bail from the third Test and
that it was presented to Bligh by the captain of
Melbourne Cricket Club's wife after England had won
the series 2-1. (Australia won a hastily arranged fourth
Test but it wasn't considered part of the series and only
had Test status conferred upon it later.) The second theory has it that the urn contained the remains of a ball
used in a Christmas game at 'Rupertswood', the country
home of Sir William Clarke (where the England team
were staying), and was presented to Bligh before the
series by one of the Ladies of the House, Florence
Morphy, a music teacher, who would later become Bligh's
wife. Neither story has been confirmed beyond doubt.

This verse appears on the side of the urn, and is reputed
to have been penned by Miss Morphy:

> *When Ivo goes back with the urn, the urn;*
> *Studds, Steel, Read and Tylecote return, return;*
> *The welkin will ring loud,*
> *The great crowd will feel proud*
> *Seeing Barlow and Bates with the urn, the urn;*
> *And the rest coming home with the urn.*

Bligh inherited the title of Lord Darnley but died in 1927. Florence, his widow, presented the urn to the MCC in the same year and it remains on show in the museum at Lord's. The ten-centimetre-high trophy has only left cricket's HQ twice, on a museum tour of Australia coinciding with the country's Bicentennial celebrations in 1988, and for England's 2006-07 defence of the Ashes down under.

The 'Bodyline' tour of 1932-33 simply highlighted the fact that the teams would try anything to emerge victorious in a series, particularly now that the Ashes were at stake. Where the tour brought home the dangers of fast, short-pitched bowling to unprotected batsman, it also brought about massive slanging matches between the two countries in the media. The Australians were furious about the leg theory tactic as it nullified their star batsman Donald Bradman, though he still managed to average over 50 in the series.

England captain Douglas Jardine refused to buckle to the media pressure and let his fast bowlers do their talking on the pitch. Aussie skipper Bill Woodfull was struck a fearful blow below the heart, wicketkeeper Bert Oldfield had his skull fractured by a bouncer and Stan McCabe had to plead with his mother not to attack the bowlers if he was hurt. At this point the Australian Cricket Board decided to intervene, sending a telegram to the MCC:

"Bodyline bowling is causing intensely bitter feelings between our players as well as injury. In our opinion it is unsportsmanlike. Unless stopped at once, it is likely to upset the friendly relations between England and Australia."

England's bowlers kept up the assault and went on to take

the series 4-1, but, bodyline bowling having been out-lawed, they were not good enough to trouble the 1948 'Invincibles' either on or off the pitch, the incomparable Bradman in the twilight of his career still proving too strong. By 1958-59 England arrived in Australia with a great chance of returning home with the urn but Ian Meckiff's rather dubious bowling action turned out to be unplayable and Peter May's side were soundly beaten (4-0).

Ray Illingworth's 1970-71 team were determined to stop the rot; they hadn't won the Ashes since the home series in 1956. Fast bowler John Snow was so fired up that he subjected the Australian batsmen to a barrage of short-pitched bowling and eventually bounced one off tail-ender Terry Jenner's unprotected head. 'Bodyline' was the word shouted by the crowd and the contest descended into farce. Snow was bombarded with beer cans by the crowd on the Sydney Hill and then attacked by a drunk. Illingworth tried to restore order by approaching the crowd and pleading for calm but he was eventually forced to lead his team from the field. They only reappeared when the match referee warned them that they would for-feit the match if they refused to play on. Snow went on to take 31 wickets in the series and England retuned home triumphant (2-0). This series revitalised the contest as a spectacle and paved the way for its continued success in the next millennium.

England struggled against the fast bowling of Jeff Thomson and Dennis Lillee throughout the 1970s and Australia dominated the next three series. Lillee's most controversial moment involved his batting, however. In December 1979 he walked out to the middle in Perth with an aluminium bat. It was within the rules to brandish such a weapon but every time he struck the ball the noise

THE GROUNDS

Name/Date	City	Capacity	First Test	Number of Tests
Lord's (1814)	London	30,000	1884	112
Edgbaston (1882)	Birmingham	21,000	1902	43
Headingley (1899)	Leeds	15,000	1899	65
Trent Bridge (1899)	Nottingham	15,358	1899	53
Old Trafford (1857)	Manchester	22,000	1884	70
The Oval (1845)	London	23,500	1880	88
MCG (1853)	Melbourne	99,000	1877	100
SCG (1848)	Sydney	43,649	1882	95
Adelaide Oval (1871)	Adelaide	32,000	1884	65
W.A.C.A (1890)	Perth	22,000	1970	34
The Gabba (1895)	Brisbane	42,200	1931	49

Note: Not all records were set during Ashes contests.

echoed round the WACA like a broken church bell. England captain Mike Brearley objected on the grounds that it was damaging the ball, as well as his team's ears! The umpires agreed and Lillee was forced to swap to the more traditional willow, but not before he'd hurled the metal bat across the pitch in a fit of petulance.

In 1977 a match was held to commemorate the centenary of the first Test between the two countries. Australia won by 45 runs, exactly the same result as in the original match.

England dominated the contests fought during the early 1980s, Ian Botham's heroics in 1981 ushering in their few

Highest Score (Innings)	Best Bowling (Innings)
333 (1990) Graham Gooch (Eng)	8-34 (1978) Ian Botham (Eng)
285* (1957) Peter May (Eng)	7-17 (1902) W Rhodes (Eng)
334 (1930) Don Bradman (Aus)	8-43 (1981) Bob Willis (Eng)
278 (1954) DCS Compton (Eng)	8-70 (2006) Muttiah Muralitharan (SL)
311 (1964) Bob Simpson (Aus)	10-53 (1956) Jim Laker (Eng)
364 (1938) Len Hutton (Eng)	9-57 (1994) D Malcolm (Eng)
307 (1965) Bob Cowper (Aus)	9-86 (1978) Sarfraz Nawaz (Pak)
287 (1903) R Foster (Eng)	8-35 (1887) G Lohmann (Eng)
299* (1932) Don Bradman (Aus)	8-43 (1894) A Trott (Aus)
380 (2003) Matthew Hayden (Aus)	8-24 (2004) Glenn McGrath (Aus)
226 (1932) Don Bradman (Aus)	9-52 (1986) Richard Hadlee (NZ)

* denotes not out

years of superiority. But with Allan Border at the helm the Australian sides of the late '80s toughened up considerably, both physically and mentally. Sledging the weaker English reached new heights or depths, depending on your point of view, and both Gooch's and Atherton's sides were comprehensively beaten. Mark Taylor's sides continued to torment the English throughout the '90s and Steve Waugh made sure their stranglehold lasted well into the new millennium.

By the time of the 2005 series, England had enjoyed a resurgence in form and were high on confidence. They'd dispatched Zimbabwe, Bangladesh, New Zealand, West Indies (home and away) and South Africa (away) and entered the summer with the weight of expectation upon them. Michael Vaughan's team didn't disappoint. Despite being soundly beaten in the opening Test at Lord's, they recovered magnificently to take the greatest Ashes series 2-1.

The team performed poorly in Pakistan in the winter but came through the Indian leg, showing a return to form by winning their first Test there since 1984 and squaring the series. Tough home series against Sri Lanka and Pakistan helped prepare the side for their biggest test, the 2006-07 tour to Australia, and the chance to retain the Ashes…

There have been 295 Ashes matches before this winter's tour of Australia, and, of the 63 rubbers contested, Australia lead 34-29. Of those 295 Tests they have also won more – 116 to 95 – with 84 having been drawn. (There were nine matches played between the two countries between 1876 and 1882 before the Ashes concept, and another five have been played without the urn at stake since 1976.)

"He's twisted his ankle and is in excruciating pain.
It's especially bad as he's here on his honeymoon. Still, he'll
probably be alright tomorrow if he sticks it up tonight"
Brian Johnston

"Cunis: that's a funny name, neither one thing or the other"
NZ commentator

"The bowler's Holding, the batsman's Willey"
Brian Johnston

"He didn't quite get his leg over"
Jonathan Agnew

IT'S A FUNNY OLD GAME: II

England's wicketkeeper Alfred Lyttelton was instructed by W.G. Grace to bowl for a spell in the 1884 Ashes contest at The Oval. Grace went behind the stumps and caught Billy Midwinter first ball. Lyttelton then proceeded to mop up the Australian tail with four wickets for just eight runs!

Australia's Charlie McLeod can consider himself unfortunate to be dismissed in the first Test at Sydney in 1897. He'd scored 26 when he was bowled by a no-ball. Not hearing the umpire's call – on account of his deafness – he began marching back to the pavilion and was run out by England 'keeper Bill Storer. He had his revenge soon enough though. In the series he averaged over 55 with the bat and took ten English wickets at just 23 apiece.

In January 1902 Australian batsman Clem Hill made consecutive Test scores of 99 (the first time this had happened in a Test match), 98 and 97. Though he fell just short of three figures each time, Australia won the series 4-1 to retain the Ashes.

Sheffield United's Bramall Lane hosted the third Ashes Test in 1902.

In 1912 the Ashes were included as part of a three-way tournament also involving South Africa.

Australia's 22 stone giant Warwick Armstrong downed half a pint of whiskey to ward off the effects of malaria during the 1920-21 home Ashes series. He then scored three centuries in four Tests, took nine wickets, and saw his side win the series comfortably (5-0).

During the infamous 'Bodyline' tour of Australia, Bert Oldfield—the home side's wicketkeeper—edged an attempted pull shot into his temple off the bowling of Harold Larwood. Though the crowd was incensed, Larwood himself rushed over to see if the batsman was alright. Medical evidence suggested Oldfield was lucky to survive the resulting bone splinter, but, despite this, the two men became firm friends, Larwood helping to carry the Australian's coffin in 1976.

Australian fans organised a testimonial for English batsman Eddie Paynter after he discharged himself from a Brisbane hospital – having been diagnosed with acute tonsillitis during the crucial 1932-33 Ashes decider – and then scored a magnificent 83. In his second innings he hit the winning runs, sealing victory with a huge six.

As Don Bradman stepped out onto The Oval in 1948 he must have known that he needed only four runs in his last Test innings to end his career with an average of 100. The English team afforded him three cheers and Eric Hollies then came in to bowl. The first delivery went through to the 'keeper, but the second was a googly that Bradman didn't pick and it bowled him. No one present could quite believe it but his Test average would always remain 99.94. The master batsman played three more first class innings in England that summer, scoring 150, 143 and 153!

As a schoolboy Brian Luckhurst watched from the stands as Denis Compton hit the winning runs in the deciding Ashes Test at The Oval in 1953. In 1971 he would hit the winning runs himself as England regained the Ashes in Sydney.

England's Jim Laker took nine for 37 in the first innings and 10 for 53 in the second as the home side demolished Australia in the 1956 Old Trafford Ashes Test. Incredibly, he'd already taken a ten-wicket haul against the tourists while playing for Surrey, and his county team mate, Tony Lock, backed him up with ten Kent wickets before the end of the season. The only other time all ten have been taken by the same bowler in a Test match was by Indian leg-spinner Anil Kumble against Pakistan in Delhi in 1999. (Hedley Verity took ten for 10 for Yorkshire against Nottinghamshire in 1932 to record the best bowling analysis in first class cricket.)

England's David Steele became an unlikely hero in the 1975 home Ashes series. His side had struggled to cope with Australia's pace duo of Dennis Lillee and Jeff Thomson but the silver-haired, bespectacled Northampton-shire man was seen as a number three solid enough to blunt their attack. At 10 for one it was time to see if he could cope. Not used to the home dressing room at Lord's however, Steele made his way down to the basement toilets before eventually finding his way to the pitch. Then he managed to score a half century and went on to average more than 60 for the summer. In the 1976 series against the West Indies a local butcher promised him a chop for every run he scored, perhaps regretting the offer when Steele's freezer contained 308 frozen lamb cuts!

The Headingley Ashes Test of 1981 will always be remembered as Botham's match. His magnificent 149 not out in the second innings at least gave England a chance of bowling Australia out for less than the 130 they needed to win. It had all seemed pretty unlikely with England forced to follow on after their first innings had left them 227 behind. (Bookies were offering 500-1 odds that England could turn it around and a couple of the tourists parted with £15 for a bit of a laugh.) England then struggled to 135 for seven and were still 92 short of making Australia bat again. But then came Botham's moment. He raced from 36 to his century with 15 boundaries and two singles, and with partners Graham Dilley (56) and Chris Old (29) he helped England to 356.

In reply Australia cruised to 56 for one and victory seemed assured. Then came Bob Willis's moment, a fact too often overlooked by historians recounting events. He asked captain Mike Brearley if he could bowl from the Kirkstall Lane end as, in his words, he was getting a bit long in the tooth to keep trundling up the hill. Brearley agreed and Willis thundered in for ninety minutes like a man possessed. His figures of eight for 43 ripped the heart out of the Australian line-up and England were home by 18 runs. It was only some time later, amidst the utter dejection of defeat, that the tourists realised they'd won £7,500 on the unlikeliest of bets.

TALKING BALLS II

"In the rear, the small, diminutive figure of Shoaib Mohammad, who can't be much taller or shorter than he is"
Henry Blofeld

"Unless something happens that we can't predict, I don't think a lot will happen"
Fred Trueman

"The replay, which the umpire doesn't have the benefit of, shows that he was either an inch in or an inch out"
Richie Benaud

"So that's 57 runs needed by Hampshire in 11 overs, and you don't need a calculator to tell you that the required run rate is 5.1818"
Norman DeMesquita

"He stood on tiptoe, on the back foot, and drove the ball on the off. I don't quite know how you'd describe that shot"
Ray Illingworth

"These past five weeks have passed by at the drop of a pin"
Rachel Heyhoe-Flint

"David Lloyd is speaking to his slippers"
Tony Greig

"England have their noses in front – not only actually but metaphorically too"
Tony Cozier

CHAPTER 4
ONE DAY
INTERNATIONALS

One-day international cricket was introduced in 1971 after the first three days of the third Test between Australia and England at the Melbourne Cricket Ground had been washed out by rain. Officials decided to stage a 40 over match instead, and Australia went on to win by five wickets, surpassing England's 190 in the 35th over. The success of the experiment, which attracted 46,000 fans, forced the organisers to consider this abbreviated version of the game an alternative to the long and some-times not very interesting Test match format. With a limit on the amount of balls to be faced, batsmen tended to be more aggressive, often striking the ball for boundaries and taking risky singles, which usually led to high-scoring, entertaining matches that became increasingly popular with the public.

The game differs from the Test match in a number of ways. International matches are usually limited to fifty overs per side (domestic games – such as the prestigious Cheltenham and Gloucester Trophy – may operate with a forty or sixty over version), there are restrictions on field-er placements, limits on the number of overs bowled by an individual and stricter rules on wides and bouncers. With Kerry Packer's World Series Cricket revolution in early 1979 spectators were introduced to many other

THE WORLD CUP AT A GLANCE

Year	Venue / Final	Winners
1975	England / Lord's	West Indies
1979	England / Lord's	West Indies
1983	England / Lord's	India
1987	India & Pakistan / Eden Gardens	Australia
1992	Australia & New Zealand / MCG	Pakistan
1996	India, Pakistan & Sri Lanka / Gaddafi Stadium	Sri Lanka
1999	England / Lord's	Australia
2003	South Africa / The Wanderers	Australia
2007	West Indies / Kensington Oval	....

WOMEN'S WORLD CUP

Year	Venue
1973	Birmingham (Eng)
1977	Hyderabad (Pakistan)
1982	Christchurch (NZ)
1988	Melbourne (Aus)
1993	Lord's (Eng)
1997	Calcutta (India)
2000	Lincoln (NZ)
2005	Centurion Park (SA)
2009	....

Runners Up	Score	Final Crowd
Australia	WI: 291-8, Australia: 274	30,000
England	WI: 286-9, Eng: 194	30,000
West Indies	India: 183, WI: 140	30,000
England	Australia: 253-5, England: 246-8	100,000
England	Pakistan: 249-6, England: 227	87,182
Australia	Sri Lanka: 245-3, Australia: 241-7	24,931
Pakistan	Australia: 133-2, Pakistan 132	30,000
India	Australia: 359-2, India: 234	30,000
....	....	....

Winners	Runners Up
England (279-3)	Australia (187-9)
Australia (100-2)	England (96-8)
Australia (152-7)	England (151-5)
Australia (129-2)	England (127-7)
England (195-5)	New Zealand (128 all out)
Australia (165-5)	New Zealand (164 all out)
New Zealand (184 all out)	Australia (180 all out)
Australia (215-4)	India (117 all out)
....	....

innovations for the shorter game. The teams wore coloured clothing, used a white ball and played some matches under floodlights at night. Television audiences benefited too. Stump microphones broadcast the banter at the crease and slow-motion television replays upped the tension by showing contentious catches and close run out decisions on big screens.

A few changes to the Test match laws have been made for the fifty-over game:

The team batting first has fifty overs to post an innings score. Either they use all fifty overs or the innings is closed with the fall of ten wickets.

Bowlers are restricted to ten overs each unless the match is affected by rain and shortened.

The team batting second aims to score more than the team batting first within the allotted overs.

Regardless of the number of wickets taken, if the runs scored are level at the end of the overs, the game is declared a tie.

Where the match is shortened by rain or deteriorating light a method of revising the target score (see opposite) has been introduced. It is known as the Duckworth-Lewis system.

For the first ten overs (from July 2005), nine fielders must be inside the fielding circle (30 metres from the wickets), with two in catching positions. Two five-over 'Power-plays' may then be used at the fielding side's discretion, where the same rules apply, but which does not include designating the two catchers.

Trial regulations allowing substitutes were discontinued in March 2006.

Duckworth-Lewis

Frank Duckworth and Tony Lewis devised this method of calculating a target score for a team batting second if the match was affected by rain or bad light. Other target predictors had proved unsatisfactory as there were so many variables (run rates, wickets remaining, bowler/batsman confidence etc) affecting play. The method bases its target prediction on the availability of the two resources (balls remaining and wickets left) to the batting side. The combination of these two resources is factored into the first team's batting performance and a target score is predicted. As the game has progressed, and scores have increased, D/L tables have been updated, most recently in 2004. It remains the most satisfactory way of deciding a match and has been approved by all ODI ranked nations at the request of the ICC.

Such was the appeal of the shortened game that a one-day international tournament was held in England between eight countries in 1975 and called the World Cup. The competition was so well received that the eight major Test playing nations voted to hold a similar event every four years.

"Jim is such a snob that he won't travel in the same car as his chauffeur"
Brian Johnston

"I hope the umpires aren't going by the clock on the old pavilion as it's got no hands on it"
Henry Blofeld

OUCH!
ON-FIELD CRICKETING INJURIES

In 1624 Jasper Vinall died after being accidentally struck with a bat while he was chasing a ball during a match in Sussex. Henry Brand was killed in the same manner in 1647. During the game's development batsmen were allowed two attempts to hit the ball, the first often deflecting the ball into the air. While the fielders went for the catch injuries were common, as the batsman was then allowed to play his second shot.

Frederick, Prince of Wales, is reported to have died of complications from a cricket ball strike in 1751, though how accurate this story is remains open to debate. Some historians have it that the ball might have burst an ulcer in his mouth and led to septicaemia, while others believe he died from a burst abscess in his lung.

Father of the county game in England, Alfred Mynn had been hit on the ankle in a South versus North match in 1836. Despite the pain he scored 21 not out and then 125 not out. During the 125 he was repeatedly hit on the legs and injured ankle by fast bowler Sam Redgate. By the end of the match his leg was black and swollen and surgeons almost had to amputate the limb.

Immediately after the infamous Bodyline tour, the England team faced a West Indian side full of pace and aggression at Old Trafford. Their bowlers had obviously been studying leg-theory because they subjected the home batsmen to some pretty hostile short-pitched deliveries. England toured the West Indies the following year

and Manny Martindale broke the tourists' captain (R.E.S Wyatt)'s jaw in Kingston, Jamaica. He never fully recovered from the blow.

While batting for New Zealand against South Africa in Johannesburg in 1953 Bert Sutcliffe was hit on the ear by a Neil Adcock bouncer. He was taken to hospital by ambulance but collapsed twice on the way. The teams blamed the pitch, its uneven bounce being cited as the contributory factor. Indeed five Kiwi batsmen were hurt. Incredibly, Sutcliffe returned later in the innings, head wrapped in bandages, and smashed three sixes on his way to a not out fifty.

Karachi's young wicketkeeper Adbul Aziz died after being hit in the chest during Pakistan's 1959 match against the Combined Services. It was discovered later that he had a congenital heart complaint.

In the early 1960s Indian batsman and captain Nari Contractor was seriously injured by a blow to the head. Sir Frank Worrell, captain of the hosts West Indies, helped save his life with a blood donation.

New Zealand's Ewen Chatfield was hit on the head by a Peter Lever bouncer in the mid-1970s and his heart momentarily stopped. Thankfully he was revived immediately.

Glamorgan's Roger Davis was almost killed by a hit on the head in 1971 in an incident that gave rise to the use of protective gear for the close-in fielders and helmets for the batsmen.

In the fifth Ashes Test at Adelaide in 1979, Warrick 'Rick' Darling was hit in the chest by a short-pitched delivery from England's Bob Willis. He fell to the pitch and his chewing gum lodged in his throat, stopping his breathing. John Emburey stepped in and helped the now unconscious Darling to breathe before he was taken off on a stretcher.

Australia's Terry Alderman had to leave the field after dislocating a shoulder in Perth in 1982, not, as you might expect, having held a brilliant diving catch, but after rugby tackling a streaker who'd come on to the pitch to celebrate England reaching 400. He missed the remainder of the series.

England wicketkeeper Paul Downton was hit in the eye by a bail after John Emburey had bowled Julian Wood in

1990. He retired shortly thereafter on the advice of his doctor.

England's fast bowler Syd Lawrence shattered a kneecap during his delivery stride against New Zealand in 1991.

Raman Lamba was killed by a blow to the head while fielding at forward short leg in Bangladesh in 1998.

Brian Lara was attempting to snatch a single in Kandy when he collided with Sri Lankan fieldsman Marvan Atapattu and dislocated his elbow. But in 1999 the crowd saw something even worse happen on the same ground. Australians Jason Gillespie and captain Steve Waugh collided painfully when trying to make the same catch off Mahela Jayawardene. Waugh suffered a broken nose and Gillespie a broken leg. Both were taken to hospital by helicopter.

On 21 July 2005, on the first morning of the Lord's Ashes Test, Steve Harmison served up some extremely hostile bowling. By the time he'd hit Australian captain Ricky Ponting on the helmet grille (which drew blood and required Ponting to have treatment), he'd already battered Langer's body and hit Hayden on the head.

"Welcome to Worcester, where you've just missed seeing Barry Richards hitting one of Basil D'Oliveira's balls clean out of the ground"
Brian Johnston

IT'S A FUNNY OLD GAME: III

Australia had just retained the 1964 Ashes when they headed across the Channel to play a Dutch side in a one-day game. 15,000 turned up to watch this routine victory for the tourists but they were soon in trouble and only managed 197. The home side struggled too but eventually found themselves needing 20 off the last twelve balls. The runs came up in just four balls, Onstein smashing Bob Cowper out of the ground to win the match. The West Indies, too, have had some trouble against supposedly inferior opponents. They took on Ireland in Dublin in 1969 and made 25 all out. Ireland went on to win the match by nine wickets!

South African batsman Graeme Pollock scored 222 not out for Border in a sixty over match against eastern Province in 1974, and this having only come to the crease in the twelfth over! Surrey's Ali Brown broke this record in 2002, smashing 268 off just 160 deliveries against Glamorgan at The Oval, an innings that included 12 sixes and 30 fours.

England rattled up a big score in their opening fixture of the 1975 World Cup against India at Lord's, Dennis Amiss top scoring with 137. Sunil Gavaskar's reply with the bat for the visitors was uncharacteristic. He defended virtually every ball throughout the run chase and finished on 36 not out after India's 60 overs, this despite repeated efforts from team mates to rouse him. There has never been a satisfactory explanation for this legendary go-slow.

The famous Australian Chappell family will be remembered for their invaluable contribution to world cricket, but one match involving two of the brothers left a sour taste in the mouth. Their best of five World Series Final against New Zealand was into its third rubber – with the scores at one each – when the controversy began. Captain Greg Chappell appeared to have been caught when on 52 but, with the umpires both checking for run outs and unable to give a decision on the catch, and the batsman not taking the fielder's word, he stayed out in the middle. Australia went on to register a score of 235 from their 50 overs. New Zealand replied well and eventually found themselves needing six from the last ball to tie. Greg walked over to brother Trevor who was bowling and issued some instructions. Trevor then bowled a sneaky underarm ball or 'grub' that was impossible to hit. The crowd of 53,000 was incensed and Kiwi batsman Brian McKechnie launched his bat down the pitch. The ball provoked an international incident, with Kiwi Prime Minister Robert Muldoon calling it an act of cowardice and linking the comment to the colour of the Aussie shirt.

England's Allan Lamb was one of the game's great practical jokers, usually at the expense of legendary umpire Harold 'Dickie' Bird. Bird had been laid low by a fever during the 1987 World Cup in India and was lying in bed when Allan Lamb decided to visit. Instead of bringing a crowd of well-wishers, Lamb lined up six army guards as a firing squad, telling them to "Put the poor bugger out of his misery." He would also set fire to Bird's newspapers (usually while he was reading them) and once set fire to the umpire's dressing room having locked Dickie inside. Flustered, but determined not to be beaten, Dickie escaped at the end of the match to find his car jacked up on bricks with a message wishing him a safe journey home tucked under the wipers.

Then there are the two mobile phone stories: Ian Botham forgot to leave his in the pavilion and gave the phone to Dickie out in the middle. The umpire recalled it ringing at least three times with various messages from his business manager and wife, among others. And Allan Lamb handed his to the umpire in 1990, with instructions to answer it if it rang. Dickie was none too impressed but finally agreed to look after the phone. Lamb was slow getting off the mark and then the phone rang. Dickie answered it, only to hear Ian Botham shout: "Tell Lamby to play a few shots or get out!"

One occasion when Lamb did play a shot is unlikely to be remembered fondly by the umpire. The ball deflected off the non-striker and into Dickie's chin, knocking him out!

Only two men have scored a century and taken five wickets in a one-day international. Sir Vivian Richards managed the feat against New Zealand in 1987 (119 and 5-41) but England's Paul Collingwood bettered these figures in 2005 against newcomers Bangladesh (112 and 6-31). Richards also holds two notable world records: the most Test runs in a calendar year (1,710 in 1976) and the fastest Test century (56 balls).

In 2006 South Africa hosted Australia in a one-day series. The score was 2-2 going into the final match at the Wanderers (Bull Ring) stadium in Johannesburg. Australia batted first and piled on the runs, scoring a world record 434-4 off their fifty overs. South Africa replied, reaching 433-8 before the beginning of the final over. Then Andrew Hall was caught and Brett Lee only needed to take one wicket with the last three balls for Australia to win. Incredibly, Mark Boucher rotated the strike and smashed the winning runs off the second to last ball of their allotted overs. They finished on 438-9, the world record falling for the second time in the day! The total runs scored (872), sixes (26), fours (87) and Australian Mick Lewis's bowling analysis of ten overs for 113 runs were also world records, the latter probably not worth celebrating!

"And England win by a solitary nine runs"
Frank Bough

"On the outfield, hundreds of small boys are playing with their balls"
Rex Alston

"This bowler's like my dog: three short legs and balls that swing both ways"
Brian Johnston

"Bill Frindall has just done a bit of mental arithmetic with a calculator"
John Arlott

"Pollock is such a good bowler—it hasn't even taken him a single delivery to get it on the spot"
Robin Jackman

"Yes, he's a very good cricketer but it's a pity he's not a better batter or bowler"
Tom Graveney

"And Ray Illingworth is relieving himself at the pavilion end"
John Arlott

CHAPTER 5
TWENTY 20

This shortened form of one-day cricket was introduced in 2003 – as a replacement for the Benson & Hedges Cup – to try and broaden the appeal of the game. (There are usually substantial cash prizes to be won if anyone in the crowd catches a six.) A limit of twenty overs per side ensures that the scoring is fast and furious. Wickets and boundaries are celebrated with rousing music to add to the occasion, and the theme from the movie *Jaws* echoes around the ground while the players await a decision from the third umpire. The matches themselves only last for about three hours and a result is guaranteed. These last two changes allow families to take children after school and floodlights ensure the game can be played well into the evening. As the fifty over, one-day game brought about minor rule changes and innovations, so to does the twenty over format.

- If a bowler oversteps the popping crease and delivers a no ball, the batsman may treat the next ball as a free hit and may only be dismissed run out.
- The umpires may award five-run penalties for rule infringements and time-wasting.
- Any incoming batsman has only ninety seconds to reach the middle.
- The fielding side must complete their overs in 75 minutes or face a six-run penalty for every over completed after the time limit has expired.
- A bowler may bowl no more than four overs.

Fielding restrictions include a) A maximum of two fielders beyond the circle during the first six overs, b) A maximum of five fielders beyond the circle thereafter and c) No more than five fielders may be on the leg side at any one time.

In some games players' nicknames may appear on their shirts.

Occasionally the two captains will have microphones and will be able to communicate with the commentary team to help describe the action.

A bowl-off will occur if the match is tied. Five bowlers will deliver two balls at an unguarded set of stumps, the winner being the side that hits the most. If the result is still tied, sudden death will decide the outcome.

English county sides all field teams with nicknames (e.g. Yorkshire Phoenix, Gloucestershire Gladiators). Surrey Lions won the inaugural cup in 2003. They were followed by Leicestershire Foxes in 2004, Somerset Sabres in 2005 and the Foxes again in 2006. Indeed the players often have their nicknames on their shirts, and as they walk out to bat their favourite music and other stats are listed for the benefit of television viewers.

The game has proved immensely popular in its first three years, with sell out crowds being drawn to matches in all the cricket playing nations. If the game's popularity continues to rise there is every chance of a twenty over World Cup competition being introduced.

"Boycott, somewhat a creature of habit, likes exactly the sort of food he himself prefers"
Don Mosey

CRICKETING KNIGHTS

Name / Year knighted

Sir Maharajkumar Vizianagram (India) 1937

Sir Pelham Warner (Eng) 1937

Sir Donald Bradman (Aus) 1949

Sir Jack Hobbs (Eng) 1953

Sir Henry Leveson-Gower (Eng) 1956

Sir Len Hutton (Eng) 1956

Sir Frank Worrell (WI) 1964

Sir Learie Constantine (WI) 1969

Sir Garfield Sobers (WI) 1975

Sir George 'Gubby' Allen (Eng) 1986

Sir Richard Hadlee (NZ) 1990

Sir Colin Cowdrey (Eng) 1992

Sir Clyde Walcott (WI) 1994

Sir Everton Weekes (WI) 1995

Sir Alec Bedser (Eng) 1996

Sir Conrad Hunte (WI) 1998

Sir Vivian Richards (WI) 2000

NEW TECHNOLOGY: HAWK-EYE

The Hawk-Eye system was conceived by Dr Paul Hawkins in the 1990s and made it onto our television screens in 2001. It uses six cameras mounted around the ground's perimeter to track the ball's trajectory once it has been bowled, and is said to be accurate to within five millimetres. These cameras feed their images into a computer, which then translates the data into a 3-D graphic

of the action on an artificial pitch in CGI. With so many
camera angles used, it is possible to track the ball in flight
and after it pitches (from any angle), enabling analysts
and viewers to understand the variations in line, length
and speed employed by fast bowlers, and the amount of
spin and drift imparted on the ball by the slower men.
The system can also predict the path of the ball if it had-
n't connected with the batsman's pads, which can help
commentators discuss contentious LBW decisions. After
the match, bowlers can see where they pitched the ball, if
they strayed off line, how much swing through the air
there was, and how much seam or spin they got from the
pitch. It can be a useful tool for batsmen, too. They can
pinpoint their best areas for scoring, decide if they're
stronger or weaker on one side of the wicket, and analyse
how and why they got out. For these reasons, Hawk-Eye
is now seen as a valuable training tool. It works in tandem
with the audio tape (snickometer or 'snicko' for short),
which can provide data on whether the batsman edged
the ball or whether it actually brushed a thigh pad or arm
guard before being taken by the 'keeper. Umpires always
have the final say on decisions, and they will continue to
make mistakes. Some fans believe that they should be
helped by the available technology – to eliminate all
errors – while others believe our human failings make the
game more enjoyable.

The BBC realised that Hawk-Eye would be equally effec-
tive providing information to tennis fans, and introduced
the system at Wimbledon in 2003. It is now used at all
major tennis tournaments. As of 2005 the system was
approved for use by tennis umpires to adjudicate on close
line calls, with the players' permission.

MERLYN

Another of the latest innovations comes in the form of the artificial bowler called Merlyn. Traditionally, English players have struggled to master the great spin bowlers like Shane Warne and Muttiah Muralitharan. Essentially a programmable bowling machine, Merlyn was developed by Henry Pryor as a training aid to help the England team prepare for the wide variety of deliveries offered by the spinners.

Andrew Strauss found the machine particularly helpful in his bid to overcome Warne's dominance in the pair's clashes. And the other English batsman praised Merlyn as they wrested the Ashes back from Australia. The next generation of the machine will feature a projection of the bowler on a screen with a hole in the picture where the ball is to be released. It will also be able to simulate flippers, sliders, doosras and zooters, googlies and chinamen, as well as all types of swing, seam and pace bowling. The hole in the image will allow the batsmen to watch the bowler run up, enter the delivery stride and then actually bowl. A team at Loughborough University found that a batsman was able to read a delivery much better if they were able to analyse the bowler's approach rather than just having a ball launched at them from the machine.

"And now it's over to Rex Alston for some balls"
Brian Johnston

"There's going to be a bowling change and we're going to see Afaq at the Nursery End. Now it's over to Old John Arlott at Trafford"
Rex Alston

CHAPTER 6
FOR CLUB & COUNTY

The first match between teams from different counties took place in 1709 (Kent v Surrey), but this was actually just a game across county borders and didn't comprise the best players from each region. It was a popular idea however, and in the following half century representative sides from the counties – which took their names – played each other throughout the summer. Surrey, Sussex and Kent emerged as the strongest southern areas, while Nottinghamshire posed the only serious threat to that dominance from the north.

As cricket's appeal grew nationwide during the middle years of the nineteenth century, and the Industrial Revolution saw a national rail network emerge, it became increasingly popular for sides from opposite ends of the country to challenge one another to matches. Though football and rugby were also spreading their wings, cricket came to be associated with competitive North-South contests around 1850.

In 1862 the MCC listed a strict qualification system for players to be deemed eligible for their county, should it become part of the then unofficial 'championship' (the word itself being popularised by the press). By 1873 nine leading clubs had drawn up a list of qualification rules and had increased their number of summer matches from an average of about eight to nearly thirty. The press then began to publish county results and tables but made no distinction between first class and minor matches. Though Gloucestershire was not one of the prominent counties initially, by 1876 Grace's all-amateur side had contributed to the game's popularity and ensured their standing had elevated considerably.

Middlesex's blend of amateurs and professionals took the game to a new level in 1878 and they were crowned (unofficial) county champions, though this was a title bestowed upon them by the newspapers and there was no tangible reward. By 1880 sides were actively competing for this title and the number of inter-county games doubled to more than fifty. Then, during three separate meetings in 1890, representatives from the counties formally introduced a Championship, and, more importantly, a set of guidelines and rules on how to decide it. This idea was extended in 1894 to include another five counties, which meant each side playing a minimum of sixteen games a season.

The interwar years were dominated by Yorkshire and their indomitable batsmen, particularly Herbert Sutcliffe and Percy Holmes. As the Second World War approached a new hero, young opener Len Hutton, backed up the more experienced men. Bowling-wise Nottinghamshire were perhaps the dominant force of the late 1920s and early '30s. Harold Larwood and Bill Voce would not only torment county defences but also the Australians during the same period.

"Well I shall remember that catch for many a dying day"
Brian Johnston

COUNTY CHAMPIONS
(Since two division format introduced)

Year	First Division	Second Division
2000	Surrey	Nottinghamshire
2001	Yorkshire	Sussex
2002	Surrey	Essex
2003	Sussex	Worcestershire
2004	Warwickshire	Nottinghamshire
2005	Nottinghamshire	Lancashire
2006	Sussex	Surrey

Since 1890 Yorkshire have scored 30 outright wins,
Surrey 18, Middlesex 10, Lancashire 7 and Kent 6.
Durham, Gloucestershire, Northamptonshire and
Somerset have never won a championship.

IT'S A FUNNY OLD GAME: IV

In a low scoring fixture in the 1820s, Diseworth batted
first and were all out for 1. That run proved decisive,
however, as Kegworth were all out without scoring!

A one-armed team played a one-legged team in April
1867. One-legged opener Murphy was dismissed for a
duck, but it was the manner of the dismissal that catches
the attention. He was run out looking for an ambitious
single!

In a United Willesden versus Wood Green match in 1872
Charles Absolon dismissed nine of United's batsmen in
each innings. He made sure of victory by catching the
remaining two players.

In the Nether Stowey versus Bishops Lydiard match in 1874, all the home batsmen were clean bowled in just twenty-eight deliveries. Opener C. Routley carried his bat for nought, the entire team managing just two runs.

In 1875 swallows halted a county game, as did a hovering seagull in 1885 and a swarm of midges in 1913. Flying ants and gnats interrupted play in 1935 and six players needed hospital treatment after being attacked by a swarm of bees in 1981.

In the Nottinghamshire versus Surrey match in 1887, Surrey slumped to 115 all out in their first innings, but the home side only managed 89 in reply. With the visitors cruising in their second innings at 264 for five, their captain John Shuter made a curious decision. He realised they had plenty of runs on the board but – as this was before declarations were introduced – knew his team hadn't time in the three day match to dismiss the home side again and win the match. So he ordered his team to have a slog and then deliberately get themselves out. (Shuter set the example by hitting ten runs in two balls and then knocking over his own stumps.) The rest of his side followed suit, the last seven wickets falling for just 25 runs. The Surrey bowlers then had time to skittle the home side and they won at just after six o'clock in the evening.

Club side Kildare's two reserve teams (Second XI and Third XI) were due to play Crescent of Hampstead and Crofton of Streatham respectively, on the same day in August 1899. Kildare were late arriving at their own ground and the two visiting teams mistook each other for them, tossed a coin and started playing. There was clearly a difference in class, however. Crofton managed 152 while Crescent only managed nine, seven of which were extras.

The googly was invented by Middlesex spinner Bernard Bosanquet (it is still called a 'Bosie' in some parts of Australia) and was first tried by the bowler against Leicestershire in 1900. He'd made 136 while at the crease and was feeling confident that his new delivery would unnerve the opposition when they came in to bat. Sam Coe had made 98 by the time Bosanquet was thrown the ball. No matter how much it turned the wrong way, it was probably the fact that the delivery bounced four times that confused the batsman.

Nottinghamshire's George Gunn had to be woken by his wife on the second morning of a home match in the early part of the 20th century. Her words: "You should get to the ground, George, you're 63 not out." He raced to the ground and continued his innings, performing so well that he was handed an envelope afterwards by an important-looking official. But Gunn placed it in a pocket and forgot about it. He only found it having turned up to pre-season training the following year. It was an invitation to tour Australia with England the winter before!

The Warwickshire-Hampshire match in Birmingham in June 1922 is noteworthy for perhaps the biggest turn-around in the sport, even putting Headingley 1981 in the shade. Warwickshire made 223 in their first innings but Hampshire struggled, making just 15 runs in 40 minutes, eight players getting ducks. Following on, they proved runs were available, scoring a massive 521, George Brown hitting 172 after his first innings failure. Set 314 to win, Warwickshire were bundled out for just 158.

Somerset stragglers were set 302 to win by Royal Naval Barracks at Devonport in the summer of 1922. With one over left they were well-poised at 300 for seven. The first three balls yielded a solitary run before Cornish took a hat-trick and the game was tied!

Batting for Hythe Brewery against the Police in 1925, Percy Chapman scored 183 out of his team's total of 201, eleven of which were extras. Eight team mates failed to score.

Playing for Aberdeenshire against West Lothian in 1939, Alma Hunt took seven wickets for 11 runs and the entire team were dismissed for 48. Hunt, opening the batting and carefully rotating the strike, then scored all 49 runs needed to win!

It is said that Australia's Keith Miller deliberately allowed himself to be bowled by Essex in a tour match in 1948 because he was on a winning streak at cards against team mates in the pavilion. His side were bowled out in just six hours, though by then they'd rattled up 721 runs!

A politicians side took on an actors side in 1955. The MP for Knutsford, Lieutenant-Colonel Bromley-Davenport, skied a ball towards Richard Attenborough, but the actor misjudged its flight and the ball hit him in the face, requiring him to spend two days in hospital!

In 1959 Pakistan and Karachi's star batsman Hanif Mohammad ran himself out playing Bahawalpur on the last ball of the day when he was on 499.

Ralph Lindsay took a hat-trick for Port Elizabeth against Oudtschoorn in South Africa in 1957, bowling Voges, Jones and Le Grange. In 1963 he repeated the feat, the second hat-trick coming in the same annual match, with the same batsmen bowled out in the same order!

In 1965 Warwickshire captain and wicketkeeper Alan Smith took the unusual decision to bowl himself after his depleted line up (Test match call-ups being the problem) failed to make a breakthrough in the Essex batting order. Dennis Amiss put on the gloves and watched from behind the stumps as his captain returned a spell of six overs, six maidens and four wickets, which included taking a hat-trick.

Nottinghamshire's Garry Sobers became the first man to hit six sixes in an over, the feat recorded off the bowling of Glamorgan's Malcolm Nash at Swansea in 1968. Bombay's Ravi Shastri is the only other man to achieve this in first class cricket, his maximum over coming against Baroda in 1984. Nash, incidentally, was also hit for five sixes and a four by Lancashire's Frank Hayes in 1977.

In a South Australia-Western Australia match in 1969 Greg Chappell was bowling to John Inverarity when the ball cannoned off a swallow and into the stumps. Fortunately the umpires declared it a dead ball (and bird) and the batsman went on to make 89.

Sussex were heading for a home win over Surrey in 1972 in that they needed just 18 runs from 18 balls to reach their target of 205. And they had only lost one wicket.

Then the ball was thrown to Surrey off-spinner Pat Pocock. He took wickets with his first, third and sixth deliveries and Sussex stumbled to 189 for four. At the end of Robin Jackman's next over, however, they needed just five to win. Pocock completed his hat-trick with his first two deliveries, then took another wicket with his next, a stumping, and yet another two balls later. Then a run out occurred on the last ball of the match and the game was drawn. Pocock had taken a world record seven wickets in eleven balls.

When the tides permit, which is usually only for a couple of hours in March and September, a game can be played on Bramble sand bank in the Solent. In 1984 the Royal Southern Yacht Club scored a six off the last ball to beat The Isle of Wight's Island Club with seconds to spare.

Schoolboy cricket can't match the standard or intensity of the first-class arena but Hurstpierpoint's Mark Payne took a scarcely believable haul of nine wickets for nine runs against Seaford in 1988. Even more impressive is that all his victims were clean bowled!

As West Indian batsman Brian Lara heard the death rattle of his stumps going down at Edgbaston in 1994 he started for the pavilion thinking he was out for just ten. But it was a no-ball. He was almost on his way a few balls later for eighteen but wicketkeeper Chris Scott dropped a sitter, then remarked that he hoped Lara wouldn't go on to make a century. By the end of the day Lara had already broken one world record when he registered his seventh hundred in eight innings. Partner Trevor Penney eventually fell for 44 and a stand of 314 was over. As Lara brought up his 325 his season average crept over 200. He

TALKING BALLS III

"There is Neil Harvey with his legs wide open waiting for a tickle"
Brian Johnston

"We owe some gratitude to Gatting and Lamb who breathed some life into a corpse which had nearly expired"
Trevor Bailey

"That black cloud is coming from the direction the wind is blowing, but now the wind is coming from where the black cloud is"
Ray Illingworth

"And I can see a strong wind blowing the sun towards us"
Brian Johnston

"It's Friday evening here. The first Test between England and India starts next Wednesday at 4 am, so nip upstairs now and set your alarms for that one"
Charles Colville

"And that's Dickie Bird standing there with his neck between his shoulders"
Brian Johnston

"If Gower hadn't caught that it would have decapitated his hand"
Farokh Engineer

survived a chance – dropped at square-leg – while on 413. Records continued to tumble as he approached the highest individual first-class score, Hanif Mohammad's 499 made in 1959. On 497 a bouncer struck him on the helmet and then he smashed the next delivery for four to register the first ever quintuple hundred.

In the 2004 Hollybush Tavern versus Capel match, home batsman Richard 'Beast' Beastall smashed 85 runs from 22 scoring shots and only had to run the odd five.

OUCH! II
OFF-FIELD CRICKETING INJURIES

Mercurial England captain Ted Dexter was involved in a 'hit-and-not-going-anywhere' incident in 1965 when his own Jaguar ran him over in London. He was pinned to a door with a broken leg and blood running down the street according to one passer-by.

England's Chris Old seemed particularly injury prone during the 1970s, but even he must have been surprised to sneeze and miss the next Test with damaged ribs.

Derek Pringle was sorting through a list of friends he'd like to invite to the 1982 Headingley Test match against Pakistan when the back of his chair collapsed. He suffered back spasms and missed the encounter.

Sussex's Ian Greig broke his house key in his front door and then tried to break in instead. He succeeded in falling eighteen feet from a window and breaking his ankle. In another instance of misfortune/stupidity he ended up colliding with an X-Ray machine while waiting for a scan on a broken finger, the resulting wound requiring a couple of stitches.

On England's 1993 tour to the West Indies, Leicestershire's Chris Lewis shaved his head and suffered heatstroke as a consequence. He missed the tourists' first match.

West Indian Jimmy Adams supposedly sliced open his hand while trying to butter a bread roll on the flight to South Africa in 1998. The rumour mill says he was trying to calm down arguing team mates instead. He flew home immediately and missed the tour.

South African wicketkeeper Mark Boucher severed tendons in his hand while trying to dice some meat in his hotel while on the 2000 tour of Australia.

England's Mark Butcher can consider himself one of the unluckiest of cricketers. In 2004 he cricked his neck in a car crash and then he sprained his wrist lifting weights. He hasn't played for England since.

CASH IN CRICKET

1611: Group of teenagers fined for playing in Sussex.

1654: Three Kent men prosecuted for playing on a Sunday. They are fined two shillings.

1664: The Gambling Act limits stakes to £100, a small fortune in the time of Charles II. The sport is funded by bookmakers for the next century.

1677: Thomas Dacre, Earl of Sussex, is paid £3 to attend a match.

1694: An unidentified man places a bet of two shillings and sixpence on the outcome a of a match in Lewes, Sussex.

1697: A Great Match is contested – also in Sussex – between eleven players, with fifty guineas as prize money.

1751: The Earl of Sandwich offers £1,500 to the winners of the England-Old Etonians match at Newmarket. £20,000 is wagered on the outcome.

1760: John Nyren notes that all matches played at Hambledon attract stakes of over £500. Gate money is usually twopence.

1813: Thomas Lord rents two fields in St John's Wood for £54 per year.

1827: A match between Sussex and All England at Darnall is played for 1000 Sovereigns.

1838: A single-wicket match between Alfred Mynn and James Dearman attracts a purse of 100 guineas. 5000 spectators turn up to watch.

1857: A match at Kirkstall, Leeds, between James Sadler and John Grange (with each allowed one fielder) attracts stakes of £50 per side.

1884-85: In the second Ashes Test in Melbourne, Australia use eleven different players to those fielded in the first Test. They refused to play unless offered half the gate receipts, which was seen as an unacceptable arrangement.

1891: Lord Sheffield donates £150 so that a shield can

be contested by Australian state sides. He also offers
financial backing to the 1891-92 tour providing that
W.G. Grace plays, which is a condition imposed by
Australian manager Harry Boyle. Grace agrees, not
surprising as his personal appearance fee amounts to
£3,000, some £100,000 by today's reckoning. The final
cost is £16,000 but gate receipts recoup £14,000.

1893: England's Maurice Read nets £1,200 during his
benefit match.

1895: The Daily Telegraph urges readers to salute W.G.
Grace's immaculate form (he completes a century of
first-class hundreds and averages 51 for the season) by
sending in a shilling apiece. £9,000 is raised. The fee
for playing for England is £10.

1896: Five English Test players demand a £20 match fee
for The Oval Ashes clash, Grace's expenses proving the
catalyst. Three players back down and play anyway but
Billy Gunn and George Lohmann are dropped.

1936: 4,000 turn up to watch a match between Bert
Wensley and Bill Ashdown, and an eleven from the Isle
of Oxney, with all the proceeds going to charity. The
Oxney XI manage 153, despite the fact that there are no
other fielders apart from bowler and wicketkeeper.
Ashdown and Wensley then make 186, knowing that a
single wicket would have ended their innings.

1937: Australian Clarrie Grimmett does himself and Vic
Richardson out of more than £1,000 when he bowls
Don Bradman on the first day of their benefit match.
If he'd managed to stay in for another hour, the ground
would have filled to capacity with 40,000 spectators
who'd just finished work for the week.

1973: Cambridge University play non-stop for twenty-
four hours – under floodlights during the night – and
raise £170 for charity.

1975: Sponsors Prudential inject £100,000 into the
inaugural World Cup held in England. West Indies
get £4,000 for winning. Ashes hero David Steele's

testimonial nets him £25,000.

1983: Clubs and players to share £1,000 fine for bowling overs too slowly.

1988: Lloyds of London refuse to insure the Ashes urn on its museum tour of Australia, citing the object as a priceless artefact.

1990: David Gower and John Morris are each fined £1,000 during the Ashes tour because they leave the ground during the match against Queensland to take rides above the stadium in antique bi-planes.

2001: Mark Butcher is fined £1,000 for staying out too late before a Test against Australia at Headingley.

2003: The Cricket World Cup in South Africa turns a profit of $194 million, up from $51 million in 1999. Winners Australia take home $2 million.

2005: ICC invests £1 million to develop Kenyan cricket.

2006: Central contracts worth more than £250,000 a year to top twenty English players.

"Well Pietersen wasn't even into double figures –
he'd only scored fifteen"
Charles Colville

"He's got perfect control of the ball right up to the
moment where he lets it go"
Peter Walker

"It's been a fabulous day for England in Mumbai
but not for England. Let's go back there now to celebrate
with England"
Charles Colville

TALKING BALLS IV

"Kapil Dev seems to have a preconceived idea in his head, but he doesn't seem to know what it is"
Tony Lewis

"The Sri Lankan team have lost their heads – literally"
Gamine Goonasena

"The obvious successor to Brearley at the moment isn't obvious"
Trevor Bailey

"Well, Wally, I've been watching this match, both visually and on TV"
Ken Barrington

"The hallmark of a great captain is to win the toss at the right time"
Richie Benaud

"After their 60 overs the West Indies have scored 244 for 7 all out"
Frank Bough

"He'll certainly want to start by getting off the mark"
Don Mosey

"He's a very dangerous bowler – innocuous if you like"
David Lloyd

"And we have just heard, although this is not the latest score from Bournemouth, that Hampshire have beaten Nottinghamshire by nine wickets"
Peter West

REFERENCE

I consulted a number of sources when writing this book.
They are listed below.

www.cricmania.com
www.cricinfo.com
www.wikipedia.com
www.howstat.com.au
www.reference.com
www.sholay.com
www.dangermouse.net
www.334notout.com
www.abc.net.au
www.abcofcricket.com
www.lords.org
www.cricbuzz.com
www.answers.com
www.bbc.co.uk/sport1
www.google.co.uk
www.cs.purdue.edu
www.faqs.org
www.radioacademy.org
www.hinduonnet.com
www.icc-cricket.com

Sky Television
Channel 4 Television
ESPN's Legends of Cricket

Classic Cricket Clangers by David Mortimer
Cricket's Strangest Matches by Andrew Ward
The Ashes' Strangest Moments by Mark Baldwin
Ashes Victory by The England Cricket Team
Cricket – A Way of Life by Christopher Martin-Jenkins
The Sledger's Handbook by Liam McCann

I would like to thank Ashley Gaunt, Seamus McCann, Darren
Thompson, Rachel Harrison, Simon Metcalf, Mark Payne, and
Mark and Stuart Turner.

This book is dedicated to the memory of Selina Young,
writer and artist of extraordinary ability.